The Mental Handbook

The Guidebook To Approaching
Sports and Life With a Bulletproof
Mindset

D1445855

Introduction

"The mental is to the physical as three is to one." -
Napoleon Bonaparte

The mental game is everything. How you approach life
mentally — also know as your attitude — will have more
impact on your success than any of your physical tools
or abilities.

In life, there are many people on both sides of the
achievement spectrum. There are those who perform
well above their means. Then there are those who
achieve well below what their tools would suggest.

How these people approach the game of life, mentally,
is the main reason for each success and failure.

What I'm doing with this Mental Handbook is touching
on all the issues our minds combat in any competitive
space, which is all of life, every day.

From family doubting your ambitions; choking on the big
stage; to feelings of fear; obtaining and maintaining
confidence; trash talk, and everything in between.

Think about one of those days, games, practices or moments when your mental engine is clicking on all cylinders. You perform at your best. No matter what your body or mind is telling you, you jumped into the driver's seat.

You a message to every function of your person. Your sore and lethargic body and mind, and your wavering emotion heard it loud and clear:

"Shut up. I got this. You will follow my lead."

You instantly started to feel great, despite the circumstances, and executed at your highest level.

When it was done you felt like you could've done the whole thing all over again, right there on the spot. On your way home you wondered how that happened.

What triggered it? How did I get into that mental state and more importantly, how can I get back there? Can I just bottle up this feeling and save some for tomorrow?

It all seemed so random, and the stimulus that brought it on isn't there every day.

So, what's the trick to re-creating this energy? How can you do this every day?

Whether you're a basketball player, lawyer, security guard or high school science teacher, I guarantee you very well know the phenomenon I'm describing.

I'll be honest: There is no magic formula for creating this energy. If there were, someone would have written about and licensed it, generating billions of dollars already. It's worth that much.

Imagine what you would accomplish if you could have that type of mental energy every day. What would you pay for that?

Probably your entire next paycheck, because you knew you could earn it all back, and then some, with the exact formula for getting your mind to click that way. I cover this phenomenon (also known as The Zone) in this book.

One thing to understand: this Handbook is not a step-by-step how-to guide.

Do not take the principles discussed here and blindly follow them to the letter in every situation. Just as in a game of basketball, you take the skills you develop in practice, and apply them to your specific situation as needed.

Just because you have a guide, does not send your brain on vacation. What you learn here shall be applied to what you do and what you already know to be true.

Some chapters will end with "Actionables," which are actions or thoughts you can put into use right now.

Let's get to it.

Feeling Left Out Of A Group

When I first started playing basketball, every friend my age was better than me.

Neighborhood basketball tryouts came and went. I didn't make any teams, all my friends from the playground made teams.

While they were at practice or games for those teams, I was left alone at the park. This was the inflection point of my paying career.

I could either

A) *Feel sorry for being left out and not good enough, say "f*** basketball" and go do other things with my time. or*
B) *Use that alone time to develop my skills while no one was paying me any attention. The choice I made then, has made all the difference in what's happened since.*

I like crowds. I love the energy of being amongst a group of people somewhere. Concerts; the mall during holiday season; airports.

When it comes to my most important goals, however, I abhor crowds. Because if I find myself amongst the crowd when working towards any goal, something isn't right.

The crowd is where average people hang out. Right there in the middle, fitting in, doing what everyone else is doing. Thinking, talking and acting in ways that are acceptable by the crowd, so as not to draw too much attention to yourself, and be accepted. Herded together like sheep. You can't tell one from another.

Blended in. Accepted as "normal". Not drawing any attention. Just like the rest of them. That's what average means.

When you're a part of the crowd, you're the average.

None of us will be the greatest at *everything*, so there are moments to be in the crowd. When it comes to your most important aims, however, the crowd is the last place you want to be.

When NBA legend Michael Jordan enrolled at the University of North Carolina for college, UNC assistant coach (now UNC head coach) Roy Williams told Michale, he would have to work a lot harder at UNC than MJ had worked in high school.

MJ replied, "Coach Williams, I'll work just as hard as everybody else."

Roy Williams replied, "Well Michael, do you wanna *be like* everybody else?"

Actionables:

1. Decide if you want to be one of the group, like everyone else, or if you want to stand out.

2. Stand alone and set your own example, and let everyone join *your* group.

Family Doubting You

I graduated college in 2004 and moved back home. My parents asked me what I planned to do with my life, now that I had my college degree.

I told them I was going to play professional basketball. That was my vision, though I had no exact plans, and zero prospects.

I knew I'd probably start out at some 9-to-5 job in the immediate future, but my goal was still my goal: To play basketball and get paid for it. Neither of my parents had been athletes; both had worked "normal" 9-to-5 jobs all my life. Their frame of reference did not connect with my vision.

My mother, who is an educator herself and did all she could to make sure my sister and I got a solid education, wasn't too pleased to hear that I planned to play basketball after all that time (both of ours), money (mostly theirs) and effort spent on education.

Said my mother, "You have a college degree! If you like basketball so much, go play in a (local) men's league or something!"

It's not that my parents were so much against basketball, it's that they didn't understand how I could spend four years in college, get a degree, and want to pursue a career that had nothing to do with anything taught in those college lecture halls.

My mother wanted the best for me; she just had no idea that sports was a viable option. After all, I had barely made the basketball team in high school (as a senior, no less) and had had mediocre results in college at the NCAA Division 3 level. No reasonable person would've predicted "Professional Basketball Player" based on my resume to that point.

But again, my goal was MY goal.

***

We must accept that some people - even our friends - can sometimes be negative toward us, through no fault of our own.

People have their own lives and their own issues.

You could be the target of someone's negativity, though their *real* issue is in their own head. This person hasn't yet addressed that real issue, and you just happened to be in the wrong place at the wrong time.

But family is an entity we can always count on, supposedly.

Blood is thicker than water or money or egos, so they say.

Family is the rock of support we can always depend on, no matter what.

At least that's what we all would like to think.

What happens, though, when your family members are the very people telling you what you can't do?

Sometimes this shows in people's indifference. Maybe you hear outright lack of belief in your expressed. What about a parent literally not allowing you to take the necessary actions?

What do you do when family are the ones discouraging you and actively attacking on inhibiting your aspirations?

It's one thing when mom or dd is indifferent to your dreams. You can ignore them all the same and go on your way. But what about a family member taking a vested interest in discouraging you, verbally knocking you down for seemingly no reason, or for a reason they deem "better for you" than what you think for yourself?

Family members cannot be cut loose as easily as strangers or friends. You're stuck with family for life. But that doesn't mean you can't raise your level of thinking and being above their negativity.

Usually, family members do want the best for you. The challenge is, they don't always know the best way to go about that (though they may think they do). Believe it or not, there are people who think *their* way is the best way for everyone.

Maybe you have to behave a certain way around certain people, since you are living under someone's roof, being supported financially, or are legally their responsibility.

You cannot escape this reality in form (unless you plan on running away - I don't offer and tips on doing that). But you can escape this reality in your mind and your attitude, two things only you can control.

The only way you can prove you're serious about your goals, is to make your life reflect that seriousness.

Talking has proven useless, so shut up. Bide your time and let your actions speak for you, not your words.

Actionables:

1. Understand your family member may only know one way, which is what was best for him or her. It's the only way he knows! Don't fight this, just observe and understand it. Accept people for who they are.

2. Know that though you may not be able to completely separate from family, how you *think* and *feel* about yourself is completely your own choice.

3. If you don't have the means at the moment to physically separate from these people, play your role as you must, for as long as you must.

    Fighting reality will only make things worse. Strategize and plan ahead for the moment when you will have the freedom to do as you wish.

Recognize that moment when it comes, and seize it.

Friends Not Believing

Up through age 15, I was one of the worst payers in my neighborhood in my age group. I never made any of the local teams, and when I did, I didn't play much. The coaches in the area, who had only so much time and energy, had to focus on the players who showed the most promise. I was clearly not one of those players.

All of my friends played basketball; they were all better than me. They made the teams and played time in the games. They were the kids the neighborhood coaches knew and paid attention to. My friends made the teams at their middle and high schools every year.

Even though they were my friends, we were teenagers; teenagers talk s*** to each other.

I heard it all:

"You're 6'1" (or whatever my height was at the time, usually taller than the person speaking) and can't dunk!?"

"You'll never make varsity at your school!"

"You can't even make the team at Finely (our local rec center)!"

"You might as well stick to baseball, Dre. Forget basketball."

Think a stranger can be harsh? Friends can be even more treacherous.

Unlike strangers, friends are know our weaknesses and vulnerabilities from up-close. A friends can stab you in the back more easily than some random person; a friend is usually right next to you. A friend can turn on you and be your worst enemy - friends know where to hit us hardest.

Like you, I've had friends who didn't believe in me.

What's important is that you distinguish between two different types of non-believing friends.

1. The well-meaning kind who are still supporters at heart.
2. The toxic "friends" whom you need to get away from immediately.

You must discern which group each friend in your circle is in.

I've had non-believing friends who were still friends. These friends supported me and hoped I did well, even if they weren't sure my course of action would play out successfully. I kept and still have many of those friends. They meant no malice and were just expressing an honest opinion.

The other, toxic type? Get away from them, and fast.

These are people who will openly sabotage you, or try to, both mentally and physically.

They will not only tell you they don't believe in you and why, but they'll try to convince *you* of why you're not good enough.

They'll tell you why you should aim lower. They'll tell you your level should be somewhere that is, curiously, very close to where *they* are.

These people are like poison, too much of it kills you. And the more you listen to it, the more poison they're feeding to you.

Keep the poison out of your bloodstream.

Actionables:

1. Identify which friends of yours, though they may not agree with your choices, still mean well and have your happiness and success at heart.

2. Identify and remove, completely and immediately, toxic people whose presence brings your spirits down. They're a drain on your energy.

    Read the tone of their words: Are they really looking out for your best interests, or trying to bring you down?

3. Fortify your own thinking: You do not *need* your friends, your friends need you. The friends who care most about you will stick with you no matter what you decide to do with yourself (within reason).

    Your life, your choices.

Feeling Hopeless

I tried out for my school's varsity basketball team every year in high school (my school did not offer a JV program until my senior year).

I got cut each of my first three years.

I wasn't devastated my freshman and sophomore years. I wasn't that good, and deep down, I didn't expect to make it.

My junior year, though, I expected to make it. I had even started dunking regularly by this point.

1998 was MY year.

Then I went to tryouts and ended up with the worst possible situation.

I had to guard the team's returning power forward, a garbage-man type guy whose only abilities were being strong and tough. I was athletic and my basketball talent was beginning to blossom. But I was literally powerless against strong players like this guy. This was my worst possible matchup.

He abused me, scoring maybe 5 baskets in a row, right in front of the coach, all the other players trying out and a bunch of girls who'd stuck around after school to watch tryouts.

I was the big story of tryouts because of the way I'd been embarrassed that day. Over the next week, people who didn't even go to my school mentioned the tryout story to me.

There was no lower low than that.

I was a high school junior, ready to make the team and start my Michael Jordan path. But I had just been embarrassed at tryouts.

There was nothing positive — not a single thing — I could draw from that day to build upon. I seriously considered, for several days, what I would do with my life, since basketball appeared to be over.

***

We all have had these moments. Some grand plans don't happen the way we expected. We prepare for a big moment, in front of everyone — and fall flat on our faces. We watch another person get the opportunity we just *knew* was for us. There is absolutely nothing on the horizon, from the current vantage point, worth looking forward to. Just a treadmill of nothingness.

How do you get out of this?

1. Get up off your ass and move. Take a walk. Really — go outside and walk for 20-30 minutes, observing your surroundings. Doesn't matter the weather, just do it.

2. Go into your closet, basement, computer, or trunk of your car and find something that you can physically see or hear or touch that reminds you of a great moment on your life.

   You need this.

   Immerse yourself in the feelings of that time and moment. Think about what you were thinking back then. Remember how you felt about yourself then.

   Ask yourself what you have done and thought since then that's changed, and ask why.

3. Do something that puts you closer to *that* feeling, no matter how small.

    It could be ten pushups you do right there in the bedroom. Maybe walking your dog or going for a run. Talk to yourself how you talked to yourself — in your mind or out loud — back then, during that great time.

4. Watch your favorite music video or movie or TV show. Read your favorite book or website or blog post. Allow the energy of that media to sink into you. Remind yourself what made you love it.

Hope is, simply, *expectation and desire for something*. If you have a hopeless feeling, the easy way out of it is to have something to expect and something to want.

What do you want? What are you expecting? Think deeply about these. You may need to create some new wants and desires.

There's nothing wrong with pivoting and going in a new direction. As soon as you realize you're going the wrong way, get up and go the other way.

Any positive thoughts you have for the future, is your hope. Hope is what wakes you up in the morning. Find something to expect and desire. Treat it as if your life depends on it.

Because it does.

Performed Terribly On Big Stage

After being cut my junior year of high school, I played for my local recreation center's team and actually did well.

My coach designed some plays for me and I delivered. I was one of our top 2 scorers every game. We were undefeated headed into our league championship game.

The gym was packed that night. Everyone in the crowd and on the opposing team knew who I was, and I loved knowing that they knew they had to figure a way to stop me.

I was primed and ready to go. I'd envisioned my successful performance and winning a trophy — if not the MVP, at least the league championship hardware for our club.

The game started and I scored the first basket of the game with a move I had never even done before.

That first basket was the last good thing that happened for me that night.

I missed my next ten shots, and we lost for the only time that season.

I had no excuses.

I wasn't nervous or scared; our opponents' defense was not exceptional. I had just missed the exact same shots I had been making all season. There was no explanation for what had just happened.

It was a complete crash and burn.

***

You were all ready for it. Waited for the day and wished the rest of the day would just hurry up and be over, so you could get to it. Planned out everything you were going to do. Your even laid out your clothes. You were primed and ready for the big event.

And you crapped the bed. Fell flat on your face. Embarrassed yourself in front on everyone - and I mean *everyone*.

Your face burned because you could feel every eye in the building on you, and not in a good way. If there was a deep hole you could've crawled in, you'd still be in there now.

Understand this: Embarrassment is a state of mind.

No one and nothing can *make* you feel embarrassed -- you must choose to feel it.

Think of a person who's really good, at the very thing you're embarrassed about failing at. Imagine if he had had a performance as bad as yours.

How would he feel? Embarrassed? Ashamed? Not at all.

The mentality of someone who is used to being on top is simple.

"This is out of the ordinary. My allies and opponents know it, the spectators know it, I know it. I own this, and everyone knows this is not something you should come to expect. Tomorrow is a new day and I **will** be back. See you next time."

Embarrassment is a feeling, a choice. There is no circumstance in life in which you are required to feel embarrassment. You could just as easily flip it around:

"This is your one time to see me down, so enjoy it. Because you know what it is next time."

No one is perfect every single time around.

The best performers you know of have had bad turns, took losses and been responsible for serious foul-ups. You've probably seen some of them. In this sense, we are all the same.

What separates one group from the other, though, is how we respond.

Everyone on the outside will have their opinion. Opinions are not new and people with opinions will never go away.

What's *your* opinion?

You determine how you feel. You determine your response and you determine what happens next time. Was that your death knell or was it just a setup for your comeback?

Your choice.

Actionables:

1. Understand that no one will perform perfectly for every performance.

2. Remember you are one of the best, and your bad performance is an aberration, something out of the ordinary.

3. Bad performances happen to us all, but embarrassment is a choice. You must choose embarrassment. And you can just as easily deny the feeling.

The Mind Needs Pictures

I read a book in high school that had an exercise I still use to this day.

It went like this.

Picture yourself walking, and another person is coming from the opposite direction right towards you.
As you get closer, you notice this person looks familiar. That's because it's you, five years from now.
You observe the five-years-from-now You. How do you walk? How do you talk? What do you look like, how confident are you? What have you achieved? How do people perceive you? Where are you headed in life?

This is the practice of visualization. That visualizing I did back then came to be.

I liked that feeling of "seeing" who and what I would become, and I kept doing it — every day, every month, every year. Every single thing I have done and become since then, is the physical manifestation of a vision I created and "saw" myself becoming.

***

Reading books, especially this one, is cool. We learn, exercise our brains, and expand our imaginations. Reading can teach you just as much as attending school can teach you.

What activates and sticks in the human mind, however, are pictures. The brain works off of visuals, not text.

Don't close this book! I'm not saying you should depend on television and YouTube for your knowledge from now on. What I am saying is this: When you're ready to activate your mind and stimulate yourself into action, you need to translate your thoughts and ideas into images for your mind.

Pictures are to the mind what fuel is to a car or good food is to our bodies, in it's what makes them run.

Have you ever heard how an author or musical artists "paints pictures with words"? Those people are highly regarded because of an ability to translate thoughts, ideas and concepts to images, the brain's premium octane fuel for action, excitement, and feeling.

When you're ready to drill a thought, idea or action into your mind, associate that thought with a visual representation. Let it sink in, thinking about it and feeling it deep inside your psyche. Remember, your brain cannot distinguish between imagination and reality. What you feed your mind, your brain believes.

Your mind is hard-wired to match your actions to those images.

If you want to be it, see it first, and you're halfway there.

Actionables:

1. Give your mind an image of what you want to be or do, not just words.

2. Associate your ideas and thoughts with images, which translate much more clearly to your brain.

What Do You See (In The Mirror)?

When I made plans to attend my first professional basketball exposure camp, I knew I was ready.

I knew I would go there — wherever it would be — and dominate. I knew I had the ability play with any basketball player, and I knew I would impress anyone watching. I knew it was my time to make something happen for myself in the arena of pro basketball. It was the time, and I was The One.

I walked into a gym filled with 250+ players. I didn't know any of them, save for two friends I had traveled with.

Before the balls even stared bouncing, I remember telling myself, "I am the best player in here, and I am about to prove it."

I proceeded over the next two days to do just that, resulting in a strong scouting report from the scouts in attendance, along with video, which in turn led to my first professional basketball contract and the career that launched everything you know about me now.

***

For most of us, the first thing we do after getting out of bed is head to the bathroom.

Your bathroom has a mirror. When you look in your mirror, what do you see? Where you go in life, and what you do, is determined by your answer.

How you see yourself is how you'll live, simple as that.

If you see yourself as weak and powerless, your life will reflect that image. When you see the opposite, you get the opposite.

Have you ever met a person whose confidence was very much outsized of his physical accomplishments, reputation or position?

Conversely, how many people have you known whose potential and abilities are much, much higher than what he's actually achieved?

What propels the first person to see himself as so much greater than what he appears to be, and what holds the second person back?

For each, the answer is exactly the same.

What each of these people sees in the mirror determines his station in life. One person sees more for himself than his current space, and one person sees less.

How can you apply this knowledge?

Start with the story you tell yourself when you look in the mirror. Who are you? What are you capable of? What's your potential? What's your destiny?

You determine the answers to all these questions. Many people set themselves up for less, short changing their own destinies, by selling themselves short in their very answers to these questions. Don't make that mistake!

What have you been telling yourself? What can you change about what you see in the mirror? You can start right now with a new set of responses, which will change your entire outlook, and in turn, your entire being.

Actionables:

1. Ask yourself, what do you see when you look in the mirror?

2. Knowing that what you see determines who you become and how you'll live, tailor your answers to be in line with who and what you want to become.

Confidence: What It Is, And How To Get It

When I was 16 and playing on my local rec team, we lost a game at a tournament we were hosting.

I had not been much of a factor in the game. I had not been much of a factor in any of our games to that point, actually. But I felt it was time for me to become a factor, whether that meant I would be exposed as either a bum-a** player, or I would become a star contributor on the team. Either way, something *needed to happen.*

As I left the locker room, I made a comment to one of my teammates that we had lost because no one had given me the ball. One of the area coaches (not my direct coach) heard me and asked me to repeat myself. I repeated myself and walked out of the room.

A week later when the team reconvened for practice, our head coach pulled me aside and told me he had heard about my statement. He said he was going to give me a chance to back up my talk, creating some plays for me and making me more of a focal point of the offense.

For me, it was either sink or swim from that point.

I became our top scorer and our team went undefeated in the regular season. Fans in the neighborhood came to games expecting me to produce. My team expected me to deliver every game.

And I was doing it.

When I made that "give me the ball" comment, I had had no logical reason to feel that way or back it up. I had never done anything significant on a basketball court, and we had just lost a game in which I hadn't done much.

Even though I didn't know a coach would hear me say what I'd said, I'd faked my confidence at that critical moment when the coach asked me what I'd said. Just saying it alone made me more confident.

That manufactured belief got put to the test, and I'd come through with all eyes on me.

The rest is history.

***

Confidence.

Everyone has heard if it. Some have it. Some don't. We all want some amount of it; many of us want more.

What *is* confidence?

By definition, confidence is "The feeling or belief that one can rely on someone or something; firm trust." Confidence is knowing something will happen or that someone will come through.

The more important question many have, though, is how? How does a person develop confidence with nothing in their past to draw on for belief in themselves?

Follow my example. You fake it.

Get a vision in your mind of what the most confident person would do in your circumstance, and emulate it. You *become* that person.

People's perceptions of you are based solely on how you present yourself. And with your confident exterior, you will be perceived as the confident person you're pretending (for now) to be.

What happens next? The more people who perceive you this way, the more they believe it, and in turn, the more *you* believe it.

Remember the imagination-reality concept from an earlier chapter, and remember the brain doesn't know the difference between the two.

The reality manifests itself. Fake-it-till-you-make-it *does* work, when you work it.

Actionables:

1. Assume the confident pose, physically and mentally, of the person whose confidence you wish to have.

2. Believe it yourself, and watch as the people you come in contact with start believing.

3. Live happily ever after.

(Strategy Of The) Crown

We discussed in the Mirror chapter how the way you see yourself determines what you do and how you'll be perceived.

The Strategy of the Crown is about carrying yourself as if greatness is your destiny.

This theory is borrowed from author Robert Greene, who introduced the concept in his writing. The Strategy of the Crown works thusly.

Place a figurative crown on your head, and carry yourself throughout your day as if the crown has to stay there. Maintain a dignified pose at all times, never losing control of your emotions, just as a king or queen is always dignified and in control.

A king knows he is the king. He doesn't need to shout about it, or put others down to feel powerful. Nothing shakes the confidence he has in himself.

Actionables:

1. Place the Crown on your head and live your life as if the crown has to stay there forever.

Imposing Your Will

Will: The faculty by which a person decides on and initiates action.

Every human has a will. We all have the capacity to decide, and the ability to make an impact on people, places, things and situations. Some wills are stronger than others; some people never initiate the power of their own will. In any competitive environment, especially sports, the use and power of will strongly determines success.

Think of your will as the gas pedals of a car.

Once a car is started and put into drive, the car can cruise on its own without any gas. There are people you know who, live life this way (figuratively speaking). The car is started and running, but no gas is applied! These people just cruise along, getting there when they get there.

The human will is the difference between that cruising vehicle and a car driven with a "lead foot," pressing hard on the gas pedal. The harder the pedal is pressed, the faster the car goes and the more ground it covers.

Remove the the gas pedal from the nicest car on the car lot, and the car goes nowhere, even though it's a beautiful vehicle.

Your will initiates your actions, be it walking from the living room to the kitchen, or going to work every day with a focus on goals.

Without your will initiated, nothing happens.

Actionables:

1.   Understand, your will determines not only what you do, but the degree to which you do it.

2.   Instead of seeking more talent or know-how for a task, consider the engagement of your will. That alone will make the difference in your ability to get something done.

Using Teammates/Friends As Your Mental Opponent

Some teams I have played for in Europe didn't have many actual games — we'd play once a week. But that didn't make the rest of the week a picnic.

We would have practice, twice a day, all week. Ten practices for every one game.

Practicing that much with so few games, I had to find ways to get motivated every day. I started treating the practices as if they were games — winning drills, preparing mentally for practice like I would for the game.

I Competed in scrimmages as if the win meant everything. My intensity, in turn, upped everyone else's intensity, and I started anticipating the practice battles. Practice was all I had, so I treated it as such.

***

Opponents will challenge you at every turn -- it's their job as an opponent, after all, to stop you from succeeding. And sometimes the people "on your side", such as teammates and friends, can be used just as well as the people wearing the opposing uniform. When you're a competitor, you need this mental edge to keep you sharp.

You're at work or practice every single day with those same people, and you both may get sick of each other eventually.

The wrong thing gets said or done, and things happen. We often find ourselves competing with teammates anyway, for positions, salaries, favor of coaches and supervisors.

There's nothing wrong with that feeling of competition with those on your team. The practice against them sharpens you for the official games. And after all, you're there to compete. The art form here, is learning to use those allies for your competitive purposes, establishing your dominance, while still keeping your teammates strong enough wifi themselves to be depended on in the trenches of battle.

Defeat them, but don't destroy their psyche. You'll need them later.

When competing against friends and teammates, apply all of your strength while at the same time not making it personal. Making a competition personal breeds resentment; teams crumble from within when internal resentment festers.

Remember, you're using each other to sharpen yourselves for the real games, against the real opponents, and you'll need each other when it counts.

Actionables:

1. Approach your practices against your fiends and teammates as if they were games, to keep you both sharp.

2. Don't make it personal, remembering that you'll need each other in battle, when it most matters.

Approaching Work With The Proper Mindset

When you're showing up to work or practice or a workout every single day, it's inevitable there will come a day when you don't feel so motivated.

The fire just isn't burning as hot some days, and you can't get past the feeling of working "just because". This happens to everyone. The difference between people is what each of us decides to do on those days.

When I'm in the gym and don't have that "feeling" that gets my adrenaline going, I don't start my workout until I *do* get into the proper mindset.

I stay in my car or on the sideline or in the locker room until I'm ready to approach my work properly. What do I do? Read some pages from a favorite book or online post. Watch a video clip saved on my phone. Listen to a song that gets me in the right mood. Think of some situation, real or imagined, that wakes up my competitive juices.

Understand: This — the mental preparation and approach — is as much a part of the work as what you do physically.

What will do it for you? I don't know, but *you* should know. If you don't, that's OK. Now that it's been brought to your attention, you are responsible for identifying and readying your triggers for when you'll need them.

Actionables:

1. Make a habit of gathering any items - photos, songs, videos - which trigger you into your best mindset for performing.

2. Keep these items handy, and use them as often as needed.

Fear Enlarges Objects

Fear is a self-created and self-fulfilling manifestation.

Fear is created in your mind, and your mind perpetuates the fear the more it thinks about it.

Outside of your head, fear does not even exist. Fear cannot be given to you, like the common cold or chicken pox. You mind must create fear for you to feel fear.

Fear enlarges everything it pays attention to.

By having fear of taking an action, you make the outcome you're fearing even more formidable.

Your brain is your servant. Whatever you tell it to do, it does - immediately and efficiently. For example, when you're afraid of another person, your mind does its job, by agreeing with what you've told it. You will be filled with thoughts and reasons to be even *more* afraid of that person.

When you're afraid of an action, your mind gives you even more imagined reasons to be afraid. And the more you pay attention to these conscious, made-up thoughts, the bigger they become. As we discussed in the Confidence chapter where positive thought manifests itself, negative thoughts — like fear — do the same thing.

Fear is not necessarily a bad thing. Fear exists to protect us from things which can hurt us. Things such as burning flame, or a grizzly bear set to attack. We're now more domesticated than we were in our caveman days, so many factors for which fear was created have lessened. However, our sense of fear has not evolved as quickly.

So even though human life is as safe as it has ever been for us, we still have layers of fear within us that must be directed somewhere. This is how we expand fear to simple things like approaching someone or trying out for a sports team.

Even though we're unable to completely eliminate the existence of fear, we can recognize fear and control our responses:

1. Recognize when you have fear that is completely out of proportion to what you're doing. By definition, this is accounts for almost every fear

you've ever had.

2. Ask yourself, "What's the worst possible outcome I could suffer from this action?" If you can live with that worst possible outcome (which still carries only a very small percentage chance of actually happening), take action.

3. Accept your fears and act in the face of that fear anyway. Your comfort zone expands when you step outside of it and do the thing you've been putting off due to fear.

Hesitation and Boldness

Have you ever have an idea pop up in your head for something you can do immediately? What did you do with that idea?

Surely there have been times when you just did it, possibly throwing caution out the window. And there were times, also, when you stopped to think about things before acting, thus hesitating and killing the possibly opportunity.

Hesitation is a byproduct of your conscious mind. Boldness comes from the subconscious.

When you have an idea, and you act on that idea instinctively, your subconscious mind is at work. Your subconscious mind does not hem and haw, it does not use "what if…" as part of its process.

The subconscious human mind looks at the situation, sees an opportunity, and says, "Go."

When you hesitate in the moment, taking time to think about all that could go wrong, you quiet the subconscious and ask your conscious mind to join the conversation. Your conscious mind is much more reasonable and rational; it thinks things out and considers all permutations of an action.

Your conscious mind is talking to you every time you think or say "What if…" before taking action. Your conscious mind is responsible for self-doubt. Your conscious mind considers everything that could work against you or go wrong.

Your conscious mind does have its place in your life. But there are many times when your conscious mind needs to be quiet.

Bold thoughts and bold actions originate in your subconscious. Your subconscious is not completely reckless — it knows there may be obstacles in the way — but the subconscious says, "So what?" and pushes you to act anyway (remembering our fears are almost always outsized, relative to what could actually happen).

Boldness enlarges us. Confidence increases, doubts go away, people see us differently.

Let your subconscious speak to you more. You can even start consciously *telling yourself* to act boldly. It becomes a self-fulfilling prophecy.

Boldness obliterates objects in your way. Boldness, which goes hand in hand with action, leaves no room for doubt. Bold action puts people on their heels and compels them to either move out of your way or follow you. A person acting boldly leaves no time for doubt or what-ifs or hesitations.

Actionables:

1. Consciously remind yourself to practice boldness in your everyday life, starting now. Observe how the attitude pushes people back on their heels. Notice how boldness gives you energy, as you utilize the bold attitude and it becomes part of your character.

2. Suspend your always-active conscious mind (this takes deliberate, active practice) and allow your subconscious to have some say in your actions. Watch as your habitual doubts and hesitations melt away in the face of acting instinctively.

3. Practice your boldness when you have time to think before a situation — meeting new people, a negotiation, writing an email, approaching someone you'd like to meet. Notice how the bold

attitude enlarges you in your eyes and the eyes of the people you meet.

Forgetting Others' Negative Words/ Actions

When another person does or says something that hurts us it injures twice. The first is from what they did or said; secondly from the lingering thoughts in our minds of the situation.

You should know, being great requires some selfishness. Start being selfish by forgetting the negative stuff other people say or do so your mind can be occupied by more important matters.

How many times have you found yourself lost in thought about some past situation which upset you?

You started by just thinking of the incident. Then you thought of exactly what was said and done. Then you thought of what you might have said or done had you had more time to consider the satiation.

Before you know it, you feel almost as angry or upset as you were when it actually happened, as if it's happening all over again.
How often do you find yourself doing this? Stop!

Greatness is selfish. Being selfish means thinking of yourself before you think of others.

What does that have to do with forgetting the negativity thrown your way? It means you put yourself first by forgetting about that negativity, which clears space in your mind for more productive thinking.

You don't have space in your mind to share with anyone else, so be selfish with your limited capacity. This is your space and everyone else has to leave. Now.

Actionables:

1. Let things go when they're not part of your productive process. Thoughts and memories are either they are helping you build, or bringing you down. Those bringing you down must find the nearest exit.

2. Be selfish with your thoughts. When someone else says or does something to try and move in to your head, let those thoughts know: there are no available rooms.

Trash Talk

If you play sports for long enough, you're bound to come across some trash talkers. Some are good at it, some are not. Some trash talkers keep it clean, some go way over the line. Some talkers keep their talk based on the game; some want to make it personal and take the talk off the field or court.

You have a choice in how you respond to these people. This is a choice you must make if there's any form of competition in your future.

1. Trash talk in return. This is not for everyone. Trash talking is a skill; if you have to ask another person or ask yourself if you have that skill, you don't have it. And this option wouldn't be for you.

2. Deflect the trash talk. Laugh at the perpetrator. Look at him when he says stuff, make amused faces but don't play his game. Talk to your teammates, his teammates, the fans even. Talk about the trash talker, but never directly acknowledge his banter. This is the passive-aggressive response. Passive-aggression is a

something we all use when needed. You would just be making this a conscious decision.

3. Completely ignore the trash talker. Continue as if no one is talking at all. If you're not doing well in the game, the talk may continue, as he might feel he's getting to you. If you're performing well (and better than you adversary, especially), he'll quiet down quickly, out of embarrassment.

All trash talkers really want is to 1) Get themselves going with their talk 2) Get a response from you or the audience, using your/their energy for the talker's purposes.

Again, you have a choice in how (and if) you respond.

Nervousness

Feeling nervous before a game, tryout, or any event means your mind and body know something important is about to take place.

You're anxious to get started. The best cure for nervousness is action. Once the game starts and you get moving for a few minutes, everything settles down.

But what about settling down *before* the game starts?

One technique I like to use is framing, meaning you put what you're about to do in perspective.

Framing works very simply. You put the upcoming event in a frame, big or small, that settle your nerves.

If making the upcoming event seem less important calms you down, then you "frame" the upcoming event by comparing it to where you're headed. Tryouts at high school? Think about all those players playing college ball and in the NBA. By comparison, this current event now isn't as big, and you can relax some.

If making the upcoming event feel *more* important works for you, frame it in the opposite fashion.

I will assume here, that enlarging the magnitude of an event isn't a challenge for you, which is why you're looking for ways to calm yourself down.

How you frame an event should along with your mentality. Sometimes if you diminish an event too much, you lose your intensity. For some, making the upcoming event seem too important gets you all frazzled.

Your job is to find that comfortable middle ground where you know what's at stake and are mentally prepared without fraying your nerves beforehand. This particular level is unique to each of us.

What I've always liked to do is diminish what I'm about to do, thinking of the better and bigger things to come. This current event is a mere stepping stone to the big games in my future. With this mindset, I'm relaxed.

That's what works for me. You must discover what works for you. Know also, it may not be the same technique every time. Be mentally flexible.

At other times, I *want* the pressure on me -- I think realistically about how big this is (or frame it as even *bigger*), challenging myself to step up mentally and physically to the level of what's coming.

Feeling You're Not Good Enough

Sports are a competition. *Life* is a competition. There are people trying to out-do you at every turn.

As we've discussed, your mental approach will drive your physical approach. How you feel about yourself will either enhance or hinder your performance; it's your choice which one.

You need to take complete responsibility for how you feel about yourself. As discussed in a previous chapter, there are many tools you can utilize to aid your mental priming, such as pictures, music, self-talk, and videos.

Pictures: We discussed how the human brain works off of images, not words. Find the pictures that make you feel how you want to feel. These can be pictures of you or another person, place or thing — whatever works. Pictures are the best way to send messages to your brain when you need to do so fast.

Music: You know what you like. You know how certain songs and melodies make you feel. Utilize this!

Self-Talk: This is when you literally tell yourself how you feel about you. Tell yourself you are the best. That no one is better than you., That you WILL perform at a high level. Whatever it is you plan on doing, tell yourself that — and most importantly, *believe* it.

Videos: Videos are moving pictures. They work the same way as images work. The best way to work with a video is to boil it all down to a single point which you can remember and hold in your conscious mind. An entire video may not be so easy for your memory to call on when needed. So keep it as simple as possible. The last thing you want to do is too much thinking and recall. You want to be primed to just *act*.

As we have covered in several chapters, how you feel is your choice. Whether it be a feeling of greatness and invincibility, or a feeling of inferiority, you do the choosing.

If you feel you're not good enough, your first step is to work on your mind like you would work on your body. The way you think and the things you read, watch and listen to all matter. And you have 100% control over these inputs.

Take responsibility for that control.

Fear Of Mistakes

When you are on stage (figuratively speaking; the stage can be a basketball court; the front of a courtroom; hospital operating table; a college lecture hall; a podium; anywhere you do your work in front of an audience), you are the main attraction.

The audience is there to watch you do what you do; you are not there to see them. Adopt this mindset immediately, as it places you in an offensive frame of mind (*I run this!*) as opposed to a defensive frame of mind (*I hope I don't mess this up!*).

Fear of failure is already failure, in the eyes of an onlooker.

Meaning, when you're performing *not to* mess up, you're already messing up just by thinking this way.

Remember, you're the show. Everything you do is what the people came to see. When you're afraid of messing up, you'll be stiff, hesitant and thinking too much. In the moment, you want to suspend all thinking and act completely off of instinct.

There are no she thing as mistakes.

Actionables:

1. You are the show; everything you do is a part of the performance. A mistake can only mess up your work when you decide it does.

2. Remember, the audience is there to see you. Act like it and take command of the room.

The Zone

Let's get this out of the way first. There is no guaranteed, step-by-step, full proof way to enter The Zone. If there were, we'd all be in it perpetually. The Zone is a phenomenon we have all been trying to nail down for years. And as long as performing in The Zone keeps bringing people to levels they otherwise couldn't hit, we will keep trying to figure it out.

Now let's get to what we do know.

The Zone is that area of your mind where thinking is suspended. You're acting completely off of instinct, doing what you've practiced hundreds of times. Nothing -- screaming fans, coach's instructions, the actions of the opposition -- distracts you or disrupts your focus. Emotions don't get in the way.

You are the master of all that you survey.

You have a unique brain wiring. The Zone resides in your subconscious mind, which is why we cannot force ourselves into it.

Forcing things and thinking too hard are the exact opposites of what your subconscious mind does. Being in The Zone requires you to quiet your conscious mind. Stop thinking about everything, quit analyzing, stop worrying about the future or reminiscing on the past.

The Zone is completely in the moment, 100% immersed in what you're doing *right now*. Nothing else matters (there is another activity, covered in my book The Mirror Of Motivation, which requires a similar mental discipline: Meditation).

Because you have this unique wiring, you have the job of discovering and harnessing what gets you to shut your conscious mind up, and exist completely in the moment.

It could be a certain song or photograph. Maybe it's being in a certain location. It could be a thought or phrase or a favorite piece of clothing. Maybe it's an external factor, like someone saying or doing something to you that gets your mind to "click."

There is no perfect prescription for reaching The Zone, but you will know when you are (were) there. Think about what happened *before that* to get you there.

In The Zone, everything comes effortlessly.

You notice things, but you don't think about them. You don't even think about what you're doing; you've done it enough and there is nothing to think about. Just Do It. There is no emotion in The Zone, as emotions require psychic energy and would break the trance.

Nothing and no one can bother you in The Zone. Every external occurrence moves out of your way. The only thing that matters to a person in The Zone is completing the task at hand, by any means necessary.

What breaks The Zone:

- Thinking
- Emotions
- Self-Consciousness (an inward-directed form of thought)
- Talking about The Zone (as soon as the thought of being "in The Zone" hits your conscious mind, you're out of The Zone
- Focus on anything other than getting the current job done (the future or past, for example)

Reading this, you can probably guess The Zone is not limited to sports or any certain activities.

The Zone exists for everyday things too. Anyone can get there.

The Zone can happen for an extended period of time - weeks, months, an entire season. A person who goes to work every day to pay the bills and keep their lights on and food on the table for their family? That person can get into The Zone. A scientist or doctor who spends years writing a journal or discovering a breakthrough in their field? That's The Zone. An athlete who suffers an injury with an extended recovery period, and attacks rehab every day to get back on the court or field sooner?

That's The Zone.

Your Zone is unique to you. It's yours and yours only. How another person gets into and stays in their Zone will probably not work for you, the same way you may not like how another person seasons their food, or you won't like all the same music as your friends.

The Zone exists deep in your subconscious, the most "you" part of your existence. You can't explain it and you don't have to, just like no one can explain their Zone to you. Don't talk about The Zone - remember, talking about it breaks your subconscious connection.

Find what works for you and stick to it.

Motivating Teammates

You may be the best and/or hardest working person on your team or in your company.

You want, *so* badly, to have the rest of your team perform at your level. You've tried forcing and cajoling people.
You tried taking privately with people.
You've tried sacrificing your own performance to help theirs.
You've complained to your coach or boss about them.

Nothing has worked and you're out of ideas.

So, how the heck do you get teammates to raise themselves to your level?

Here's the truth: You don't.

You cannot change people. Next time you walk into your locker room or office, look around. Each of those people are going to be exactly who they are, and there is nothing YOU can do to change them.

People make permanent change only when they want to change, not when they're yelled at or punished or even when they're rewarded.

The only thing you can do as a leader, is set an example. If you want to raise the levels of your teammates, set the example by raising your level.

Eventually your teammates face a choice. They can raise their own level to meet yours, or leave the team because they can't handle your drive and intensity for getting things done.

When you're a leader, people do not follow what you say. They follow what you do.

Yeah, they'll listen when you talk, but if your actions aren't aligned with those words, your days as a leader are numbered.

In any group, whether it be 2 people or 30,000, if you want the others to do something, you must do it first. Set the example, then do it again. And again. And again.

That, and only that, is how you drive people to action.

ABOUT DRE BALDWIN

Dre Baldwin is the world's only expert on Mental Toughness, Confidence and Self-Discipline. A 9-year professional basketball player, Dre works with athletes, entrepreneurs and business professionals.

Dre has worked with Nike, Finish Line, Wendy's Gatorade, Buick, Wilson Sports and DIME magazine.

Dre has been blogging since 2005 and started publishing to YouTube in 2006. He has over 5,000 videos published, with daily content going out to his 115,000+ subscribers and being viewed over 35 million times. Dre's "Work On Your Game" show on Grant Cardone TV is consistently top-5 in views on the network.

Dre speaks, coaches and consults business professionals on mental toughness, confidence and discipline. He has given 3 TED Talks, published 7 books and has a daily podcast, Work On Your Game with DreAllDay. A Philadelphia native and Penn State alum, Dre lives in Miami.

Follow Dre -

Twitter & Periscope:

@DreAllDay

Instagram, SnapChat:

@DreBaldwin

READ MORE BY DRE BALDWIN,
INCLUDING:

Buy A Game
Mirror Of Motivation
The Super You
The Overseas Basketball Blueprint
Dre Philosophy Vol. 0
100 Mental Game Best Practices
25 Conversation Starters
55 Daily People Skills
25 Reasons To Quit Worrying

63234583R00047

Made in the USA
Lexington, KY
01 May 2017